A Quick Tour Through the Bible Workbook Part 1:
The Books of the Old Testament

By
Dr. Sheila T. Hodge-Windover

Drawings by Deborah Berridge-Thompson, MBS.
Illustrated by Stanley Hodge.
Edited by Deborah Berridge-Thompson, MBS.

Legal Notice

All attempts were made to verify the information provided in this workbook, however; neither the author nor the publisher assumes any responsibility for errors, omissions or different interpretation of the subject matter herein.

Dedication

This workbook is dedicated to two of my nephews and two of my nieces, Daniel Thompson, Joanna Thompson, Timothy Berridge and Lydia Berridge, who willingly provided me with a photo for the cover of this workbook.

Contents

Introduction

Welcome the series on a Quick Tour Thought the Bible workbook part 1: The books of the Old Testament.   This work book has lots of activities for you to learn the books of the bible, the names of the prophets as well as some of the main characters in the Bible. You will also learn one of the favorite Bible verses for each book in the Old Testament. Some of the activities include, word find, cross word puzzles, matching, fill-in- the- blank spaces, as well as drawing and coloring. All the drawings were done by my loving sister Deborah Berridge Thompson.   I hope you will enjoy this quick journey through Bible part 1 with an emphasis on the Old Testament.   So, fasten your seat belt and let's get started on the quick tour through the Bible.

Books of the Old Testament Word Find

Can you find the first five books in the Old Testament?

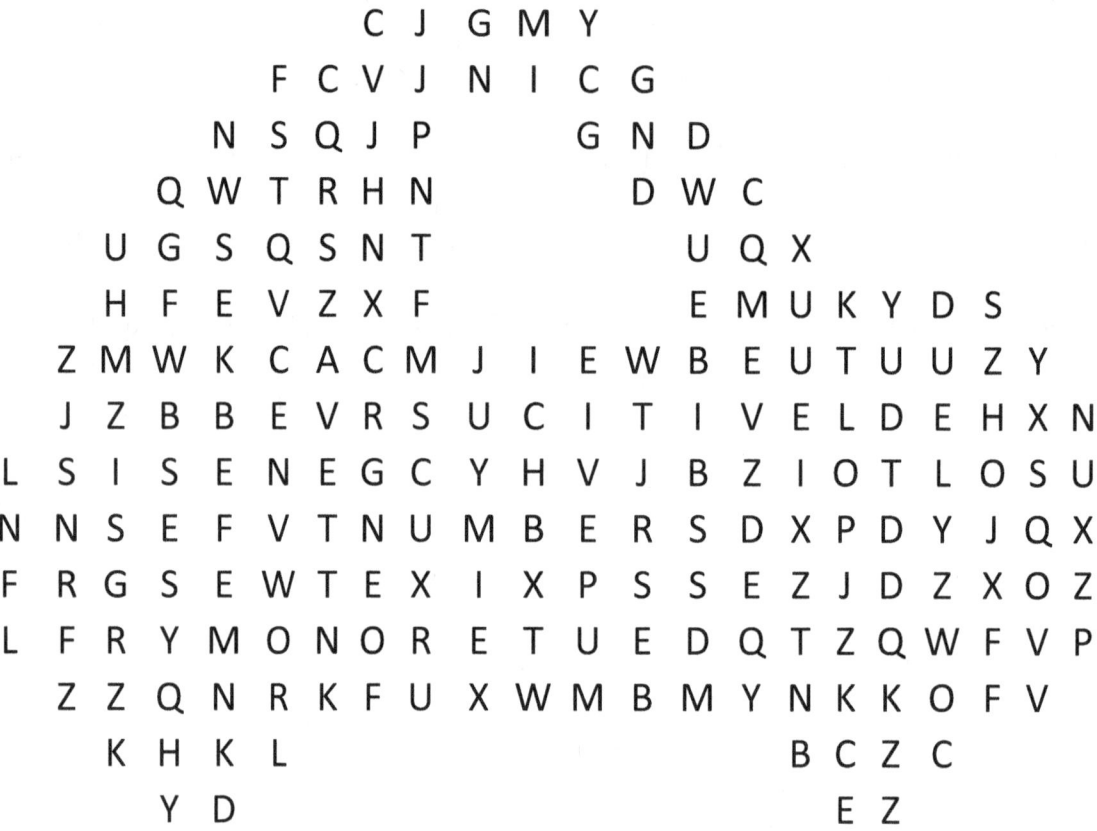

```
                    C J G M Y
                  F C V J N I C G
                N S Q J P     G N D
              Q W T R H N     D W C
            U G S Q S N T       U Q X
            H F E V Z X F       E M U K Y D S
        Z M W K C A C M J I E W B E U T U U Z Y
          J Z B B E V R S U C I T I V E L D E H X N
      L S I S E N E G C Y H V J B Z I O T L O S U
      N N S E F V T N U M B E R S D X P D Y J Q X
      F R G S E W T E X I X P S S E Z J D Z X O Z
      L F R Y M O N O R E T U E D Q T Z Q W F V P
        Z Z Q N R K F U X W M B M Y N K K O F V
            K H K L               B C Z C
              Y D                   E Z
```

GENESIS

EXODUS

LEVITICUS

NUMBERS

DEUTERONOMY

1.   How many chapters are in the book of Genesis? ____

2.   How many chapters are in the book of Exodus? _____

3.   How many chapters are in the book of Numbers? _____

4.   How many chapters are in the book of Deuteronomy? _____

How many books can you find?

```
            C H F L M
          X W Z L H V A X
        P N C R S     M W P
      D V Q T R K     D X Y
    H W H Z Q W B       I V W
    U L C W O X H       Y F G W V A B
  N R H E D D C O E A V W Y V Y V U Z J U
  P P T V S G U L U Q Z S Z O K H Q N X Y X
R L E U M A S B R I O A V F W S L C M T C M
R Q L R B Q U F H V M N X F O L R N E K D H
U P H K P T S O C U L I T J F Q O Y S O P J
F N Z E F F U Q E E T R K X J U D G E S L H
  D H D K S T L G J K W A N X W P R U Q V
    I H H I             W I Q W
      Y T               R M
```

JOSHUA

JUDGES

RUTH

SAMUEL

SAMUEL

1. How many chapters are in the book of Joshua? _____

2. How many chapters are in the book of Judges? _____

3. How many chapters are in the book of Ruth? _____

4. How many chapters in the first book of Samuel? _____

5. How many chapters are in the book of second Samuel? _____

How many books of the Old Testament can you find below?

```
            F S Z L L
          X H K H R U O G
          I Y K P K     O T K
        W F N B T I       E B E
      X H M E Q E N         A O Z
      D N C A U N G       H C R S B Y E
    C B Q H Q I W S H Q U D E X V O R A X L
    Y C C R B I D A Z B A V T Q I A P M M T N
  W H S R O T C F L M D B C K V C Q O O F M I
  A Y W D N D M P O M J O G E H R E S M A A D
  R S X U I N P W K A O Y B U E X P F V V G W
  S I Z B C L F I W K G F M E Z R A V J G E O
    W C Z L F N M U L A C H R O N I C L E S
      I A E G               O D X C
      Y S                   F L
```

KINGS

KINGS

CHRONICLES

CHRONICLES

EZRA

1. How many chapters are in the first book of Kings?_____

2. How many chapters are in the second book of Kings?_____

3. How many chapters are in the first book of Chronicles?_____

4. How many chapters are in the second book of Chronicles?_____

5. How many chapters are in the book of Ezra? _____

How many books of the Old Testament can you find?

```
            L G Y G T
          F D F N S H H M
        F L F U D       G H Y
      Y K Z U V G         P A P
    Z K S F D E D           D I B
    L I U Q S P R         P A M C I B B
  W D X P O N O O Y J D X E I S E H W J N
  G X Q U P R O V E R B S M S G U H C P O S
F Q U M E M Y N W G D E A M D N I E E D M B
V K D F R X Z Z B Z H E S E L Q E P I N K C
A I W E E V C R K M Y M M T T A I S P Z P W
H L B H F W H Y X T N X A O H M S A B O J L
  D P E Y N K R Q Q U L N N Q E P P N G N
    S O U F               L R Z J
      S F                 Z Y
```

NEHEMIAH

ESTHER

JOB

PSALMS

PROVERBS

1. How many chapters are in the book of Nehemiah? _____

2. How many chapters are in the book of Esther? _____

3. How many chapters are in the book of Job? _____

4. How many chapters are in the book of Psalms? _____

5. How many chapters are in the book of Proverbs? _____

How many books of the Old Testament can you find?

```
            O D U E K
          I N P X P R C F
        K X Q J T     S C P
      D A Q U X X     D L X
    W V U J V F B     E E S
    X M X D E C M     H V S U S K P
  H S K A C O R G H I Q X L C A I D R Z J
  H G O T B N H E I H W O A H Q K A K J M A
F P S K S T K H G M W O K E A J T C S D A G
Q U N I W F Q J Z E I F T B W P T P A T X X
X H I R C O E I V K I A D A R G F S N E E S
J Q E I H V K J H S E F H A I A S I O L J S
  V H Z D Z U S O N G O F S O L O M O N A
    G A Y D           K P V M
      B V               L D
```

ECCLESIASTES

SONG OF SOLOMON

ISAIAH

JEREMIAH

1. How many chapters are in book of Ecclesiastes? _____

2. How many chapters are in Songs of Solomon? _____

3. How many chapters are in Isaiah? _____

4. How many chapters are in Jeremiah? _____

How many books in the Old Testament can you find?

```
          L C V U U
        H O S E A W G L
      O H C P A     U V X
    V N R N D U       L L N
  T O C G Y J J         W B A
  D V K T O D F         J B I D E G K
S V R X Z H F B K A C O Q L E O J R C F
B V I R Q G P M O J Z W M M H G X E P O B
V Y D Q Y Z H B B I H C Z X O M O R Q E Q C
M P A A Z I J K L A M E N T A T I O N S V B
Q J N U W I K T W E R Z V D N U E L K P B S
K O I N L N M K E Z E K I E L F I S L X Y P
  A E Y N N O P U H U T A W T P P F U R K
    L U O Y                   N J Z S
      I R                       K G
```

LAMENTATIONS

EZEKIEL

DANIEL

HOSEA

JOEL

1. How many chapters are in the book of Lamentations? _____

2. How many chapters are in the book of Ezekiel? _____

3. How many chapters are in the book of Daniel? _____

4. How many chapters are in the book of Hosea? _____

5. How many chapters are in the book of Joel? _____

How many books in the Old Testament can you find?

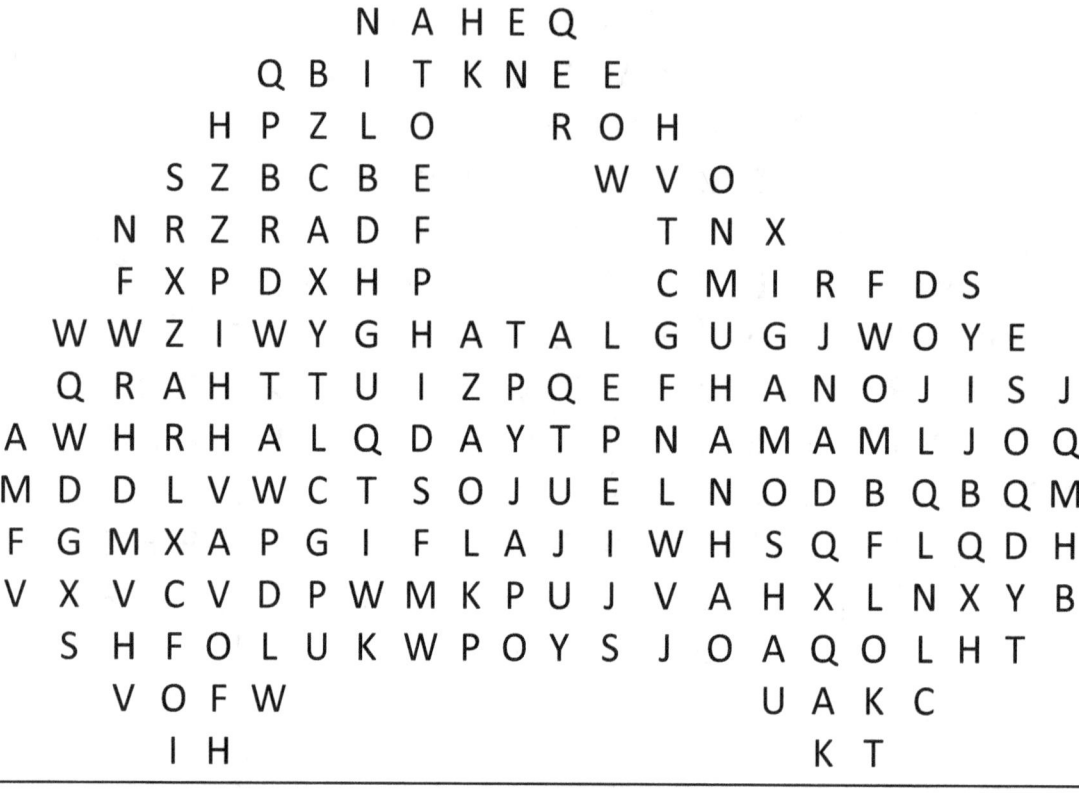

AMOS
OBADIAH
JONAH
MICAH
NAHUM

1. How many chapters are in the book of Amos?____

2. How many chapters are in the book of Obadiah?____

3. How many chapters are in the book of Jonah?____

4. How many chapters are in the book of Micah?____

5. How many chapters are in the book of Nahum?____

How many books in the Old Testament can you find?

```
        V N F S D
      H B T R I L R G
    R B H R Q     A K U
  Z Z U B P A     Q D O
  H E E B S C F     H S X
  O C P L B L Q     H M J T L H G
 D P H H J D W X O W O Q C Q S T F G S V
 C I A A A Q S B H A B A K K U K F Y P A I
O J H R N Q G L V M S W Q H Q C Z L K Q J J
F Q C I I S C G K J G H G N C U R J D V F G
J H A A A H T X A R R H L L R P T W J W W M
L J L H H G L Q B I A W E Z M K S I I B U J
 I A P S Q U H T C B D Q U C D Y H F Z I
  M H V N               C E K J
   C Z                   J T
```

HABAKKUK
ZEPHANIAH
HAGGAI
ZECHARIAH
MALACHI

1. How many chapters are in the book of Habakkuk? _____

2. How many chapters are in the book of Zephaniah? _____

3. How many chapters are in the book of Haggai? _____

4. How many chapters are in the book of Zechariah? _____

5. How many chapters are in the book of Malachi? _____

The Old Testament

```
Y O H A I M E H E N K J E R E M I A H C
M B O J I T L S E G D U J S V I J O E L
O P A H T E Z E K I E L A G S S P J E O
N O M O L O S F O G N O S N E A X O M S
O S Z J D R T W E F S E Y I L I V S O E
R M H V M I F W U H V X Z K C A I H I C
E L S H J U O F A J D O E T I H Q U H O
T A E O A W T I Y A J D Z S N V R A C N
U S A C I N N K N H T U R R O M E R A D
E P S J C A O I A M O S X I R W H M L K
D Y Y I H L E J H O S E A F H S T W A I
T J T P S L E U M A S D N O C E S O M N
M L E N J E H S O I N M F L T V E H J G
X Z X K A E N I I B C E W B S P Q P N S
G G J A G H I E C A A A I M R W V M U Z
H A G G A I U Z G O S D H V I Y Z Y M Z
F I R S T S A M U E L T I R F Z O A B W
S N O I T A T N E M A L E A I W A Z E K
E M G I A V W X E H M R E S H R T O R O
T A R Z E C H A R I A H B X O P E K S R
```

GENESIS	JOB	NAHUM
EXODUS	PSALMS	ZEPHANIAH
NUMBERS	ECCLESIASTES	HAGGAI
DEUTERONOMY	SONGOFSOLOMON	ZECHARIAH
JOSHUA	ISAIAH	MALACHI
JUDGES	JEREMIAH	
RUTH	LAMENTATIONS	
FIRSTSAMUEL	EZEKIEL	
SECONDSAMUEL	DANIEL	
FIRSTKINGS	HOSEA	
SECONDKINGS	JOEL	
FIRSTCHRONICLES	AMOS	
EZRA	OBADIAH	
NEHEMIAH	JONAH	
ESTHER	MICAH	

Old Testament word scramble

1. GISEESN   _ _ _ E _ _ S

2. XOSDUE   _ _ O _ _ S

3. VIILECTSU   _ _ V I _ _ _ _ _

4. MEUSNRB   _ _ M _ _ R _

5. OTNEOUREYMD   _ _ U T _ _ _ _ _ _ Y

6. HOSAUJ   _ _ S _ U _

7. DSEUJG   _ _ _ G E _

8. UTRH   R _ _ _

9. USA1LEM   1 _ A _ _ _ _

10. E2AMSLU   2 _ _ _ _ E _

11. GKI1NS   _ _ _ _ G S

12. N2KIGS   _ K _ N _ _

13. HELNIRS1OCC   1 C _ R _ _ _ _ _ _ _

14. LRICSCN2OHE   _ C _ _ _ N _ _ L _ _

15. ZARE   E _ _ _

16. NHEEAHIM   _ _ _ E _ I _ _

17. EEHTRS   _ _ T H _ _

18. BJO   J _ _

19. PASMLS   _ _ A _ _ S

20. RPSROBEV   _ R _ _ _ _ B _

Old Testament word scramble 2

1. HNEHAEMI   N E _ _ _ _ _ _

2. REETHS   _ _ _ H _ R

3. JBO   J _ _

4. LSPSMA   _ _ A L _ _

5. RSOBVEPR   _ _ _ _ E _ _ S

6. SLESTCCASEIE   E _ _ _ S I _ _ _ _ _

7. OGLSSOONNFOOM   _ _ _ _ _ F S _ _ _ _ O _

8. AAISIH   _ S _ _ A _

9. JREMEAHI   _ _ _ E _ I _ _

10. INNLAOMEATTS   _ _ M _ _ _ A T _ _ _ _

11. IKEEEZL   _ _ _ _ _ E L

12. IDANEL   _ _ N _ _ L

13. AEOHS   H _ _ _ _

14. LOEJ   J _ _ _

15. OAMS   _ _ O _

16. ABODAHI   _ B _ _ _ A _

17. OJHAN   _ _ _ A _

18. CHIAM   _ I _ _ _

19. AHMNU   _ _ _ _ M

20. AKBHKKUA   _ _ B _ _ _ _ K

21. ZHIHAAENP   Z _ P _ _ _ _ _ _

22. GAAIHG   H _ G _ _ _

23. HZEHACIAR   _ _ _ _ A _ I _ _

24. MHLAAIC   _ _ L A _ _ _

Sixty-Six Books Word Search

Can you find the 66 Books in the Bible

```
U T C Z I E O D J S E L C I N C R H C B G J N H O J A C T C J A F V C
G H P E K C R Y G S F H P E K A G V R W W K N E U C N J I O V F B Z Z
U K K U C H I N H A H N P C Y E Q Q B T E T Z O D S G O L O Z N L C C
O T L S B E S F A I U L X J L L G S W Y H K G Y W V S C P V U X X F C
N A F U N Z E N I U W J X Y E W Q L T X B E E Q D J E S W J C S H U A
E B Y S P E D P N N Z B C C R I N T H I A N S B O J L Y O B R E T E P
I Y C O P K W W E L H E Q U C E J O W B N P N S O V C B T I N C T H Y
H A U L V I G B R F X O P X J N T V N N N K J U A N I A L A C K P V C
H Z C K S E X F E J V Q J H B H I E O E I C N W I L N H G L L J S X U
D A R G Q L X Q J C P D K P A K P G P A L T I V Y N O N O R E T U E C
I N C C A J J X K N H N J R T N H Q O B Q I N O V H R N W W F C L U E
W R E I U H H Q B A F N A G T Y I U I C T S H F X N H P I Z J H R P N
G V B D N J B N I H R E H T S E N A P H H Z W P K Z C G S A N U E L Y
Z X C T P C Z D C A R C T N T P S U H O N C N O L C S F O G N C S U L
L E U C N K A G F G F Q H C H H H B T U B P Q N Q E U H A K N S L C F
S F V S A B L Z E V V O X T P C E S R E J C E L S N A I H T N I R C C
G X C K C T N H T X J H N S P Q L W N E C B L S N J R U Q S H T Z C P
X B A S G H A W B C N W A N W C E F Z U V I K E S N A I S S C L C C E
O F C W F B R O N E X L S I W B N I V I R C N A U S C G A G T B A T K
N A X C A B J N U Y N G A C R Z I Y J W V N R L H N N P S N L G C K B
Y X J K N Z U O H S N Z Y Z L A P V C S N Z P P C I A N X I A Q T I N
Z H K S C K N O H I K K O A F Y H A Q Y A C Q T H X A S Z K N C I L P
F U Y I Z V T I K N O T V K Y N K C H G A N C K B I N U B B E H B S C
K R E V E L A T I C N X W I E T Z T E L H L Q G S A L G S I N I I C K
L C C Z T H A I N E H E N U U X C P A Z V K A E I N W I R N T L N B E
Z X Y D S Y Y C L T G Y L K S N V T Q G A F H N S C N D P U A T A A C
K K S E T S A I S E L C C E I L I X X E Q P C H A L N E S P T K I P C
X C C D S N X O Q S V Y G T E A S V I N E L Q D I V E Y Q S I H S Z C
J L V O C C Z P W E P I A T N L K C K E A C K A A L D I K I C A V A C
E U S U T I T E C Q U E T S D H Y N O S P C R H H T N L N Z N N N C N
E V Z H G X R K T J S A V I C R Y J S I R Z A Z L V J N S A S F A S F
O C F Y L B V Y Q C U A W C C K E U S E N Z N A G B Z D C R P S A
V N L N E G T Y H I A V L G N U H B N D V C U H N L S W W K N C C A C
E C K H P G I Z F X L Z L Z F T S L L C E S R E B N U N T J G P V H T
N L N I H C A L A N R Y F B B I P N U H J P S S N A N O R E X C C U S
```

66 Books of the Bible

GENESIS
EXODUS
LEVITICUS
NUMBERS
DEUTERONOMY
JOSHUA
JUDGES
RUTH
1SAMUEL
2SAMUEL
1KINGS
2KINGS
1CHRONICLES
2CHRONICLES
EZRA

NEHEMIAH
ESTHER
JOB
PSALMS
PROVERBS
ECCLESIASTES
SONGOFSOLOMON
ISAIAH
JEREMIAH
LAMENTATIONS
EZEKIEL
DANIEL
HOSEA
JOEL
AMOS

OBADIAH
JONAH
MICAH
NAHUM
HABAKKUK
ZEPHANIAH
HAGGAI
ZECHARIAH
MALACHI
MATTHEW
MARK
LUKE
JOHN
ACTS
ROMANS

CORINTHIANS
BCORINTHIANS
GALATIANS
EPHESIANS
PHILIPPIANS
COLOSSIANS
THESSALONIANS
2THESSALONIANS
1TIMOTHY
2TIMOTHY
TITUS
PHILEMON
HEBREWS
JAMES
PETER

PETER
1JOHN
2JOHN
3JOHN
JUDE
REVELATION

Popular Old Testament Characters

Adam Eve Noah Abraham Isaac

```
                                          H  E
I  S  R  D  E  G  H  U  O  C  Z  N  X  D  O  G  A  V  V
V  H  R  V  U  L  S  F  J  B  Z  M  C  J  R  M  D  W  E
X  K                                   G  A  U  J
W  Y     X  C  O  D  Q  D  O  X  P  C  V     Y  M  U  W
F  C     A  M  D  S  Q  K  S  T  E  B  S     R  N  I  N
R  Q     S  I                 V  P     U  G  D  S
A  Q     J  Z     H  X  F  W  U     J  F     L  U  I  D
V  Y     B  X     R  P  B  X  Y     I  D     F  U  A  Y
V  V     T  V     W  Y     G  O     C  K     C  V  P  K
L  L     J  U     V  L     Q  P     V  N     S  U  O  P
M  A     V  R     D  T           D  I     Z  D  C  B
E  W     H  D     G  S  W  E  C  W  O  C     G  U  A  A
X  Y     B  G     Y  G  I  F  K  A  Q  Y     S  D  A  A
B  Q     F  H                          O  Y  S  B
E  J     E  N  F  Z  X  T  K  K  G  V  U  R  K  S  I  R
A  R     J  U  Z  C  J  N  G  C  C  W  Z  S  F  A  A
E  P                                      H  H
N  I  N  Z  F  C  W  W  V  T  Z  H  M  K  X  P  P  V  V  A
C  M  E  Y  D  F  H  A  O  N  T  I  F  U  L  S  P  V  Q  M
```

ADAM

EVE

NOAH

ABRAHAM

ISAAC

Color the cartoon below then describe the scene.

Can you find the Bible characters below?

Jacob Joseph Moses Joshua and Samuel

```
                                              D M
E V X R Z T E M X E L R W Y S M D    Z K
F B V C X M M X Q X U W S U M G Y    Q N
L G                         W X    H N
E Z   A H N G K J Z Z C N T   E E    K B
U K   J O S H U A M J N U B   N U    O O
M U   Y S             D R   S L    R C
A P   O C   I Y U K M   D D   E Y    W A
S J   S D   O E O S O   D Y   Y Y    Y J
E C   C C   L W   N M   A L   F T    J F
B I   O Y   T Q   F J   C W   K U    D M
H W   D L   W Q       B C   E T    Y E
V X   W K   D V O B H Z Z F   U B    B V
E J   H A   E L O E R B M X   Y N    S M
P J   R O             B X    Z Q
Z A   Z O T B F M E N X P S B S B    J V
O C   S H P E S O J M L B E S J Q    A F
L Q                         X Z
G E O Z C I T D Q B B T R R I Y J Z M F
I A Y M M K Z P G M O S E S N U W F N I
```

JACOB

JOSEPH

MOSES

JOSHUA

SAMUEL

Color the cartoon below. Describe what Jacob and Esau are talking about.

Color the cartoon below. Can you tell what Samuel is asking Eli?

Can you find the Bible characters below?

Saul David Solomon Elijah Ahab

```
                                                Y  D
O  A  R  G  C  U  X  T  F  M  G  P  O  M  O  I  D     W  D
V  O  R  N  D  M  R  B  S  E  P  S  M  T  N  L  W     T  F
B  G                                      X  B     H  H
T  H     K  J  I  Q  S  E  I  J  Z  O  H     S  B     F  A
F  F     K  Y  K  V  I  C  L  Y  T  D  O     N  B     K  J
K  R     B  D                 L  L     A  Y     W  I
D  L     K  F     A  X  Y  W  L     M  U     E  Z     E  L
C  T     W  S     J  X  K  L  J     V  A     U  I     P  E
Q  N     F  A     J  H     C  T     T  S     S  S     H  O
S  P     E  V     V  R     X  C     Y  R     C  O     M  F
N  B     J  J     X  O        E  I     D  L     K  V
F  M     Q  Z     Y  A  X  W  E  L  D  T     A  O     Z  Y
F  W     P  A     H  T  B  Y  K  O  Z  A     V  M     M  M
O  L     H  K                       I  O     T  T
Z  L     P  T  V  N  D  X  V  J  M  Q  L  U  D  N     R  A
V  K     T  I  E  J  W  K  T  F  H  J  H  C  O  X     G  T
K  W                                            D  O
A  R  Y  E  S  N  C  V  G  M  T  E  X  V  Y  P  A  H  A  B
P  O  J  D  N  O  B  M  K  C  H  C  E  H  K  K  V  F  G  H
```

SAUL

DAVID

SOLOMON

ELIJAH

AHAB

Color the cartoon below. Can you describe what is happening?

Can you find the Bible characters below?
Jezebel Jonah Daniel Ezekiel Jesus

```
                                        Y E
O J U J C U M O B P E Y L K Q X C     Y S
X C X C V B Q C A I U W N V N O W     H L
H B                           W X     Y H
M K   N Z F L E B E Z E J C     B P   U K
B L   G X D X X Y L Q H Y T     X H   H Z
R E   Z Y               U N     N H   B X
O L   A T   A V S K L   N G     A E   W U
A E   U E   G P Q Z Q   J C     B M   J H
U I   N Z   S U   T G   N M     V J   T Q
O K   L J   D E   G R   F C     I A   T V
G E   S F   X H       H Q       I I   E T
J Z   Y L   T D H G N U J U     S T   J C
E E   C M   J B E P K J F F     M W   R L
S O   D V                 W E   L J
U N   Y D I R I V O W K C C Q I M     O B
S A   H A N O J R B Y C M Q T D K     V E
F S                                   C G
Q O D S E I L E I N A D W I A K W M V P
N T W T H I Q C A Q I M Q Z B R I K M P
```

JEZEBEL

JONAH

DANIEL

EZEKIEL

JESUS

Color the cartoon below. Can you describe which bible character the cartoon represents?

Color the cartoon below. Can you describe which bible character the cartoon represents?

Old Testament Bible Knowledge Matching Exercise 1

Can you match the correct answer to the questions below by drawing a line?

1	How many books are in the old testament?	27
2	How many books are in the new testament?	Genesis
3	How many books are in the Bible?	Psalms
4	Which book in the bible tells of the creation story?	Leviticus
5	What is the longest book in the bible?	66
6	What is the first book in the bible?	Numbers
7	What is the second book in the bible?	Exodus
8	What is the third book in the bible?	Deuteronomy
9	What is the fourth book in the bible?	39
10	What is the fifth book in the bible?	Genesis

Books of the Bible History Matching Exercise

Can you match the correct answer to the questions below by drawing a line?

1	What is the first book in the new testament?	Solomon
2	What is the last book in the bible?	Solomon
3	Who wrote Genesis to Deuteronomy?	Revelation
4	Who wrote the book of Ezra?	Nehemiah
5	Who wrote the book of Nehemiah?	Ezra
6	Who wrote most of the book of Psalms?	Jeremiah
7	Who wrote the songs of Solomon?	Matthew
8	Who wrote the Ecclesiastes?	Moses
9	Who wrote proverbs?	Isaiah
10	Who wrote Isaiah?	Solomon
11	Who wrote Jeremiah and Lamentation?	David
12	Who wrote the book of Ezekiel?	Ezekiel

Major and Minor Prophets

Ezekiel   Hosea   Isiah   Joel   Jeremiah
Daniel   Amos   Obadiah   Jonah   Micah
Nahum   Habakkuk   Zachariah   Haggai   Malachai
Zephaniah

Do you know which prophets were the Major Prophets and which ones were the Minor Prophets?

Major Prophets	Minor Prophets

Prophets Cross Word Puzzle

Prophets 1

Across

1. Which prophet is known for prophesying about the valley of dry bones?
2. Which book speaks about the prophet who was swallowed up by a great fish?
5. Who wrote the shortest book the old testament?

Down

3. Which prophet was thrown into the lion's den?
4. Which prophet was told to marry a woman who would not be faithful to represent Israel and its behavior toward God?
6. Which prophet was most famous for being quoted by Apostle Peter on the day of Pentecost?
7. Which book that was written by a prophet has only 9 chapters?

Prophets

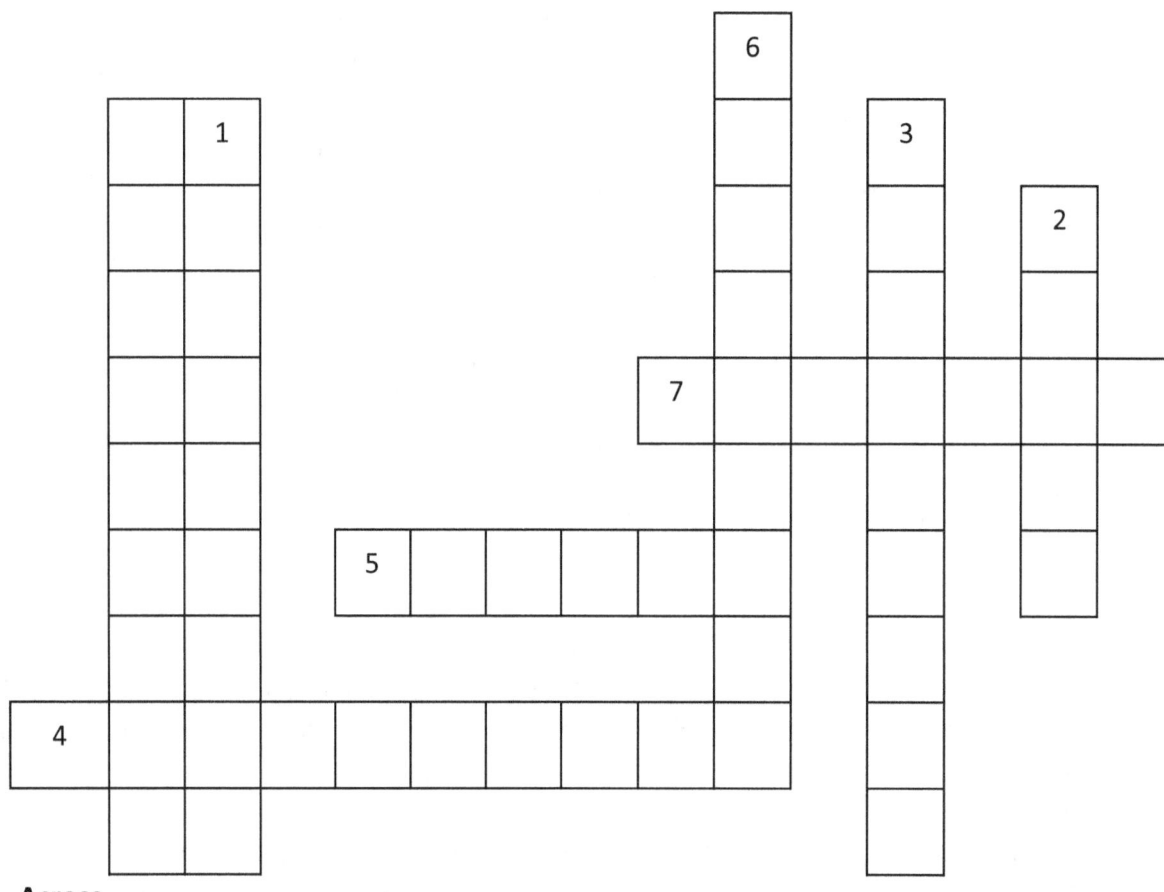

Across

4. Which book spoke about the day of the lord more than any other old testament book and the prophet prophesied during the reign of Josiah, the king of Judah?

5. Which book in the old testament written by a prophet only has two chapters?

7. Which book is the last book in the old testament?

Down

1. Which book has prophesy about the birth of Christ?

2. Which book has only 3 chapters?

3. Which book is very difficult to pronounce?

6. Which book is the second to last book in the old testament?

Popular Bible Characters Cross Word Puzzle 1

Complete this crossword puzzle to learn about some of the popular Bible characters.

Across
4. Whose name was changed to Paul?
5. Who was John the Baptist's mother?
6. What was the name of the angel who spoke to Mary?
8. How many disciples did Jesus have?
9. Who betrayed Jesus?

Down
1. Who was Samuel's mother?
2. Who was the wisest man who ever lived?
3. Who killed Goliath?
7. Where was Jesus born?
10. Who denied Jesus?

11. Who went into a sycamore tree to see Jesus?   12. Who turned water into wine?

Creation to Flood Cross-word Puzzle

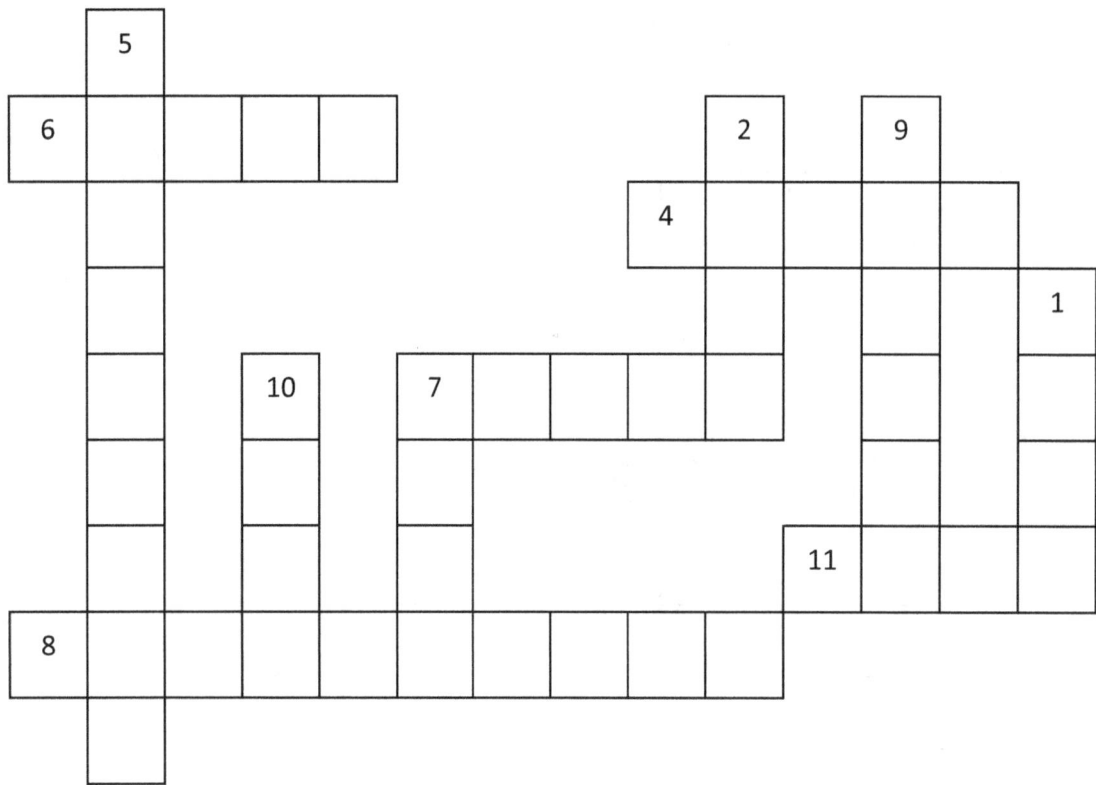

Across
- 4. – son of Enosh, grandson of Asam
- 6. – father of Enoch
- 7. – son of Jared who was taken up to God without dying
- 8. – son of Enoch, grandfather of Noah
- 11. – Noah's oldest son and original ancestor of Israel.

Down
- 1. – first man
- 2. – third son of Adam and Eve
- 5. – son of Kenan, descendant of Seth
- 7. – son of Seth, grandson of Adam
- 9. – father of Noah
- 10. – last of the ten antediluvian Patriarchs and hero of the Flood

Cain line Cross-word Puzzle

Across
1. – first man
7. – "man of God", descendant of Cain
9. – son of Lamech

Down
2. -First woman
3. – firstborn son of Adam
4. – son of Cain
5. – son of Enoch
7. – son of Irad
8. – fifth descent from Cain, rude and ruffianly, with him the curtain falls on the race of Cain

After the Flood Cross-word Puzzle

Across

2. ___father of Shem.
3. __father of multitude", the first Hebrew patriarch, son of Terah,
7. ___ original ancestor of the nation of Israel and father of the 12 ancestors of the 12 tribes of Israel.
10. __ wife of Isaac
11. ___ twin brother of Jacob
13. ___ second wife of Jacob
14. ___ only son of Abraham by Sarah and patriarch of the nation of Israel

Down

3. ___name was changed to Abraham
4. __ brother of Shem
5. ___ Abraham's wife
8. Lot's wife was turned into a pillar of ___
9. Isaac was the ___of Jacob and Esau
12. __ first wife of Jacob
14. Jacob's name was changed to ___
15. Jacob's father in-law ___

After the flood Cross-word puzzle: part 2

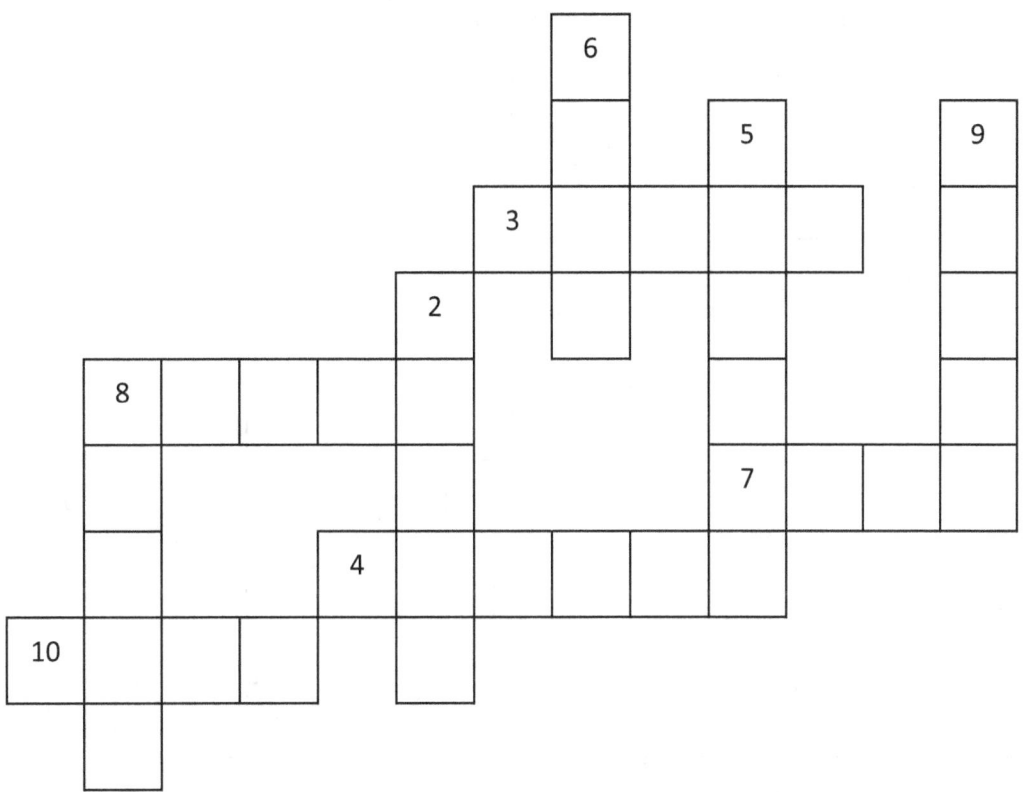

Across

3. ; Judah's daughter in law .
4. – great grandson of Jacob
7. – son of Boaz and Ruth, father of Jesse, grandfather of King David
8. – father of King David
10. ___ first King of Israel, he was king before David

Down

2. – one of the twins born through the illicit affair between Judah and his daughter-in-law,
5. – father of Boaz
6. – married Ruth and became Obed's father (David's grandfather)
8. – fourth son of Jacob and progenitor of the tribe of Judah
9. – killed Goliath

Twelve Tribes of Israel Cross-word puzzle

Across

1. Twelve Tribes of _____ (sons of Jacob, aka Israel)
2. – eighth son of Jacob and Zilpah
4. – fifth son of Jacob and the first son born to Jacob by Rachel's maid Bilhah,
5. – seventh son of Jacob and Zilpah and founder of the Tribe of Gad
6. – ninth son of Jacob, fifth born by Leah
7. _taken to Egypt as a slave, eventually became interpreter of the pharaoh's dreams
9. – son of Joseph and Asenath and founder of the Tribe of Menasheh
10. – fourth son of Jacob and founder of the Tribe of Judah
11. – third son of Jacob and Leah

Down

3. – twelfth and last born of Jacob's sons
8. – second and youngest son of Joseph and Asenath
12. – sixth son of Jacob by his concubine Bilhah
14. – second son of Jacob of Leah
15. – tenth son of Jacob and sixth by Leah

13. – first son of Jacob and Leah, founder of the Tribe of
    Reuben

Old Testament Famous Characters Matching

Exercise (A)

Match the name on the right to correct information on the left by drawing a line.

1	David	Can you name a set of twin boys?
2	Noah	Which man and woman lived in the Garden of Eden?
3	Delilah	Who was Joseph's younger brother?
4	Jonah	Who did God give the job of building a massive boat called an ark?
5	Adam and Eve	Who was thrown into a den of lions by an evil King?
6	Daniel	What was the name of the lady who was married to the strongest man?
7	Jacob and Esau	Who got swallowed by a whale?
8	Solomon	Who was known as the Wise King?
9	Benjamin	Which brave young boy had a fight with a giant called Goliath?
10	Egypt	Where was Moses born?

Favorite Old Testament Stories

Match the name to the correct information by drawing a line.

1	Shepherd	Who killed his brother?
2	Jonathan	What did God create on the first day of creation?
3	God's promise to not flood the earth ever again.	Which book of The Bible is full of wise sayings?
4	Genesis	What was the meaning of the rainbow in the sky?
5	Harp	Who made a bronze snake?
6	Proverbs	What instrument did David play?
7	Moses	What "job" did David have as a boy?
8	Cain	Who was David's best friend?
9	Moses	Which is the first book of The Bible?
10	Light	Who was given The Ten Commandments from God at the top of a mountain?

Favorite Old Testament Bible Verses

Fill in the blanks to complete these favorite bible verses

1. In the beginning God created the heaven and the _____. Genesis 1v1

2. Thou shalt have no _____ Gods before me. Exodus 30v3.

3. Thou shalt _____ _____, nor bear any grudge against the children of

thy people, but thou shalt love thy neighbor _____ thyself; I am the lord. Leviticus

19v18

4. And the ass said _____ Balaam, am not I thine ass, upon which thou has

ridden ever since I was thine unto this day? Was I ever wont to do so unto thee?

And he said, Nay. Numbers 22v30

5. _____ And Moses _____ an hundred and twenty years old when he died: his

eye _____ not _____, _____ his natural forces abated Deuteronomy 34v7

6. _____ Then spake _____ to the Lord in the day when _____ Lord

delivered up the Amorites _____ the children of Israel, and he said in the

sight of Israel, sun, stand thou still upon _____; and thou, _____,

_____ the valley of Ajalon. Joshua 10v 12

7. That he told her all _____ heart, _____ said _____ her, there hath not

come a razor upon mine head; for I have been a Nazarite unto God from my mother's womb; if I be shaven, _____ _____ strength will go from me, and I

shall become weak, and _____ like any _____ man. Judges 16v17

8. And Ruth said, _____ me not to leave thee, or to return from

following after thee: for whiter thou goest, _____ will go; and where _____

lodgest, I will lodge: thy people shall be my people, and thy God my God: Ruth

1v16

9. And Samuel said, Hath _____ LORD as great delight in burnt offerings and

sacrifices, _____ in _____ the voice of the _____? Behold, to obey

is better than _____, and to hearken than the fat of rams. _____

Samuel _____

10._____ Now therefore so shalt thou say unto my servant David, Thus saith the

Lord of hosts, _____ took thee from _____ sheepcote, from following the sheep,

to be ruler over my people, over Israel: 2 Samuel 7v8

11. Give therefore thy servant an understanding heart to judge thy people, that I

may _____ between good and bad: for who is able to _____ this

thy _____ great a people? 1 Kings 3v9

12. And Elisha prayed, and said, LORD, I pray thee, open his eyes, that he may see.

And the LORD opened the eyes _____ the young man; and he saw: _____,

behold, the mountain was full of horses and chariots of fire round about Elisha. 2

Kings 6v17

13. They were helped in fighting them, _____ God delivered the Hagrites _____

all their allies into their hands, because _____ cried out to him during the

battle. He _____ their prayers, because they trusted in him. 1

Chronicles 5v20

14. For _____ eyes _____ the LORD run to and fro throughout the whole earth,

to shew himself strong in the behalf of them whose heart is perfect toward him.

Herein thou hast done foolishly: therefore _____ henceforth thou shalt have

wars. 2 Chronicles 16v9

15. For Ezra had devoted himself to the study and observance of the Law of the

LORD, and to teaching its decrees and laws in Israel. Ezra 7v10

16. And the priest the son of Aaron shall be with the _____, when the

Levites take tithes: and the Levites shall bring up the tithe _____ the tithes unto

the house of our God, to the chambers, into the treasure house. Nehemiah 10v38

17. For Mordecai the Jew was next unto king Ahasuerus, and great among the Jews,

and accepted of the _____ of _____ brethren, seeking the

_____ of his _____, and speaking peace to all his seed. Esther

10v3

18. For I know that my redeemer liveth, _____ that _____ shall stand at the

latter day upon the earth: Job 19v25

19. Thy word is a lamp _____ my feet, and a light unto my path. Psalm 119v105

20. Trust in the LORD _____ all _____ heart _____ lean not on your own understanding; in all your ways submit to him, _____ he will _____ your paths straight. Proverbs 3v5-6

21. For _____ shall bring every work into judgment, with every secret thing, whether it be good, or whether it be evil. Ecclesiastes 12v14

22. Draw me, we will run after thee: the king hath brought me into his chambers: we will be glad and rejoice in thee, we will remember thy _____ more than wine: the upright _____ thee. Songs _____ Solomon 1v4

23. Thou wilt keep him _____ _____ peace, _____ mind is stayed on thee: because he trusteth in thee. Isaiah 26v3

24. Then shall ye call upon me, and ye shall go and pray unto _____, and I will hearken unto _____. And ye _____ seek me, _____ _____ me, when ye shall search for me with all your heart. Jeremiah 29v12-13

25. It is of the LORD's mercies that _____ are not consumed, because his compassions fail not. They are _____ every morning: great is thy _____. The LORD is my _____, saith my soul; therefore will I _____ in him. Lamentations 3v22-24

26. For thus saith the LORD GOD; Behold, I, even I, will both _____ my sheep, and _____ them out. Ezekiel 34v11

27. But Daniel purposed in his _____ that he would not defile himself with

the portion of the king's _____, nor with the _____ which he drank:

therefore he requested of the prince of the eunuchs that he might not

_____ himself. Daniel 1v8

28. When Israel was a child, then I _____ him, and called my son out of

_____. Hosea 11v1

29. And it shall come to pass afterward, that I will pour out my _____ upon

all _____; and your sons and your _____ shall prophesy, your

old men shall dream dreams, your young men shall see _____: Joel 2v28

30. Seek _____, and not evil, that ye may live: and so the LORD, the God of

hosts, shall be with you, as ye have spoken. Amos 5:14

31. Though thou exalt thyself as the eagle, and though thou set thy nest among the
stars, thence will I bring thee _____, saith the _____. Obadiah 1v4

32. And God saw their works, that they turned from their _____ way; and God

repented of the evil, that he had said that he would do unto them; and he did it

_____. Jonah 3v10

33. He hath shewed thee, O man, what is _____; and what doth the LORD

require of thee, but to do justly, and to love _____, and to walk

_____ with thy God? Micah 6v8

34. The LORD is _____, a strong hold in the day of trouble; and he knoweth

them that trust in him. Nahum 1v7

35. The Sovereign Lord is my _____; He makes my feet like the feet of

a _____, He enables me to go on the heights. Habakkuk 3v19

36. The Lord thy God in the midst of thee is mighty; he will _____, he will

rejoice over thee with joy; he will rest in his love, he will joy over thee with

_____. Zephaniah 3v17

37. The silver is _____, and the _____ is mine, saith the LORD of hosts.

Haggai 2v8

38. And he shewed me Joshua the high priest standing before the angel of the

_____, and Satan standing at his right hand to resist him Zechariah 3v1

39. For I am the LORD, I _____ not; therefore ye sons of Jacob are not

consumed. Malachi 3v6

Favorite Bible Stories in Genesis

Creation: Cross Word Puzzle

10		8	

Across

3. What did God call the darkness?
4. What did God call the firmament?
6. What did God do on the seventh day?
7. What was the name of the first man?

Down

1. Who said let there be light and there was light?
2. What did God call the light?
5. What did God call the dry land?
8. What was the name of Adam's wife?
9. What was the name of Adams first son?

10. Who killed Abel?

Noah: Cross word Puzzle

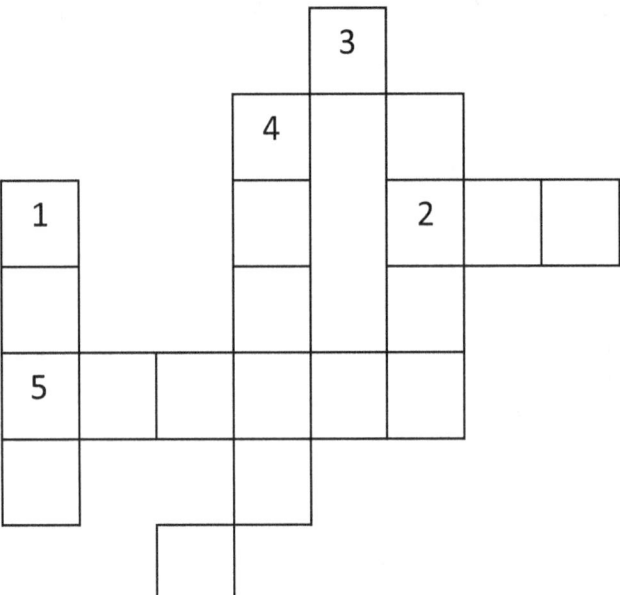

Across

2. Who shut the door of the ark?

5. What is the name of the mountain that Noah's ark rested on?

Down

1. Who built the ark?

3. How many people were saved in the ark?

4. How many days and nights did it rain?

Abraham: Cross word Puzzle

Across

3. Who was Abraham's wife?
5. What was Sarah's name before it was Sarah?
6. Who was Isaac's wife?
7. How many children did Issac have?

Down

1. Who is the father of many nations?
2. Who was turned into a pillar of salt?
4. What was Abraham's name before it was Abraham?
8. Who was the father of Jacob and Esau

Jacob: Cross word Puzzle

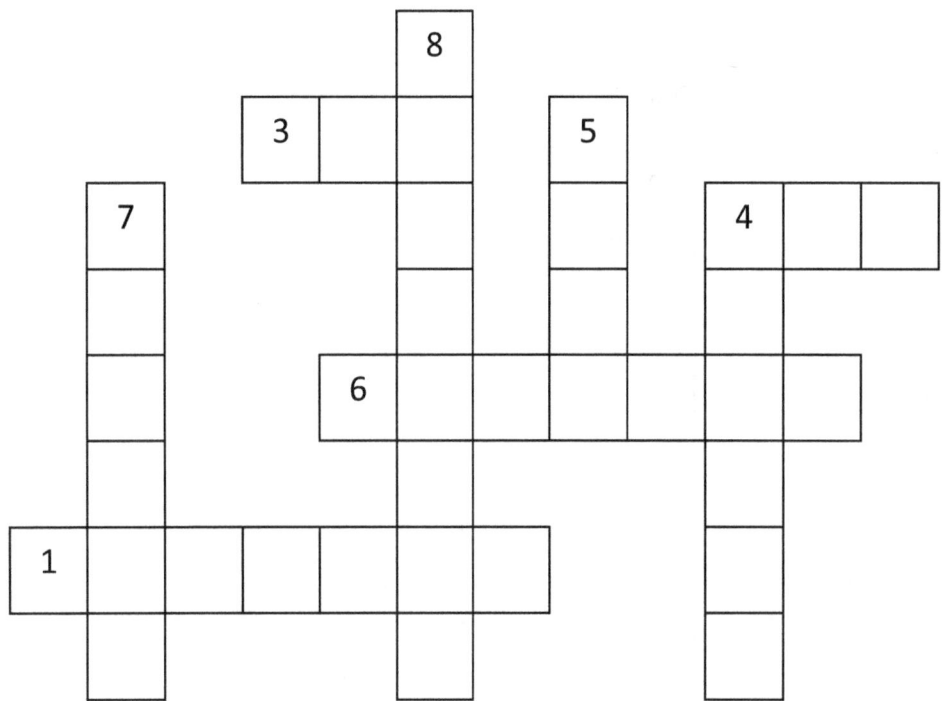

Across

1. Which book in the bible is the story of Jacob seeing a ladder?
3. How many daughters did Jacob have?
4. How many wives did Jacob have?
6. What's the name of Jacobs second wife?

Down

4. How many sons did Jacob have?
5. What's the name of Jacobs first wife?
7. What was Jacob's name changed to?
8. What was Jacob's last son's name?

Women in the Old Testament Cross-word Puzzle

Across
2. _____ is the seventh child and only daughter of Jacob and Leah.
3. _____ risked her life to save her people (the Jews), and it pays off.
5. _____ was a prophet and judge who people frequently came to for guidance.

Down
1. " She was an Egyptian princess, aristocratic, and high-born. Pharaoh honored Joseph by giving him ___ as his wife.
4. God creates _____ to be of help to Adam.

7. Hannah was barren until she meekly asked for a son from God, promising that she would dedicate him to His service.

9. _____ is the elder sister of Aaron and Moses. She suggests to Pharaohs daughter that a hebrew woman nurse baby Moses and thereby reunites Moses with his mother.

11. She was Jacob's first wife, who was deceptively given to him after he had worked for seven years

13. She is married to Isaac and is the mother of Jacob and Esau.

5. _____ name means "delicate" or "dainty one. The Philistines approach Delilah and offer to pay her handsomely if she is able to find out why Samson is so strong.

8. _____ killed the man who had oppressed the Israelites for 20 years.

10. Rachel was Jacob's second wife and his true love. She died in childbirth.

13. Joshua sends two spies into Jericho to scope out the situation. The spies find their way to hers house and she hides the men at great risk to herself.

14. ____ swears an oath, saying she will remain with Naomi.

15. Ruth and _____ both experience the loss of loved ones. ___ was Ruth's mother--in-law

16. ____ was Abraham's wife. Amazingly, she had a child—Isaac—at the ripe old age of 90.

Solutions

Solutions to Favorite Bible Verses in the Old Testament
Bible verses answers

1 In the beginning God created the heaven and the **earth**. Genesis 1v1

2 Thou shalt have no **other** Gods before me. Exodus 30v3.

3 Thou shalt **not avenge**, nor bear any grudge against the children of thy people,

but thou shalt love thy neighbor **as** thyself; I am the lord. Leviticus 19v18

4 And the ass said **unto** Balaam, am not I thine ass, upon which thou has ridden

ever since I was thine unto this day? Was I ever wont to do so unto thee? And he

said, Nay. Numbers 22v30

5 And Moses **was** an hundred and twenty years old when he died: his eye **was** not

dim, nor his natural forces abated Deuteronomy 34v7

6 Then spake **Joshua** to the Lord in the day when **the** Lord delivered up the

Amorites **before** the children of Israel, and he said in the sight of Israel, sun, stand

thou still upon **Gibeon**; and thou, **Moon, in** the valley of Ajalon. Joshua 10v 12

7 That he told her all **his** heart, **and** said **unto** her, there hath not come a razor

upon mine head; for I have been a Nazarite unto God from my mother's womb; if I

be shaven, **then my** strength will go from me, and I shall become weak, and **be** like

any **other** man. Judges 16v17

8 And Ruth said, **Intreat** me not to leave thee, or to return from following after

thee: for whiter thou goest, I will go; and where thou lodgest, I will lodge: thy

people shall be my people, and thy God my God: Ruth 1v16

9 And Samuel said, Hath the LORD as great delight in burnt offerings and sacrifices,

as in obeying the voice of the LORD? Behold, to obey is better than sacrifice, and to

hearken than the fat of rams. 1 Samuel 15v22

10 Now therefore so shalt thou say unto my servant David, Thus saith the Lord of

hosts, I took thee from the sheepcote, from following the sheep, to be ruler over

my people, over Israel: 2 Samuel 7v8

11 Give therefore thy servant an understanding heart to judge thy people, that I

may discern between good and bad: for who is able to judge this thy so great a

people? 1 Kings 3v9

12 And Elisha prayed, and said, LORD, I pray thee, open his eyes, that he may see.

And the LORD opened the eyes of the young man; and he saw: and, behold, the

mountain was full of horses and chariots of fire round about Elisha. 2 Kings 6v17

13 They were helped in fighting them, and God delivered the Hagrites and all their

allies into their hands, because they cried out to him during the battle. He

answered their prayers, because they trusted in him. 1 Chronicles 5v20

14 For the eyes of the LORD run to and fro throughout the whole earth, to shew

himself strong in the behalf of them whose heart is perfect toward him. Herein

thou hast done foolishly: therefore from henceforth thou shalt have wars. 2

Chronicles 16v9

15 For Ezra had devoted himself to the study and observance of the Law of the LORD, and to teaching its decrees and laws in Israel. Ezra 7v10

16 And the priest the son of Aaron shall be with the Levites, when the Levites take tithes: and the Levites shall bring up the tithe of the tithes unto the house of our God, to the chambers, into the treasure house. Nehemiah 10v38

17 For Mordecai the Jew was next unto king Ahasuerus, and great among the Jews, and accepted of the multitude of his brethren, seeking the wealth of his people, and speaking peace to all his seed. Esther 10v3

18 For I know that my redeemer liveth, and that he shall stand at the latter day upon the earth: Job 19v25

19 Thy word is a lamp unto my feet, and a light unto my path. Psalm 119v105

20 Trust in the LORD with all your heart and lean not on your own understanding; in all your ways submit to him, and he will make your paths straight. Proverbs 3v5-6

21. For God shall bring every work into judgment, with every secret thing, whether it be good, or whether it be evil. Ecclesiastes 12v14

22 Draw me, we will run after thee: the king hath brought me into his chambers: we will be glad and rejoice in thee, we will remember thy love more than wine: the upright love thee. Songs of Solomon 1v4

23 Thou wilt keep him **in perfect** peace, **whose** mind is stayed on thee: because he trusteth in thee. Isaiah 26v3

24 Then shall ye call upon me, and ye shall go and pray unto **me**, and I will hearken unto **you**. And ye **shall** seek me, **and find** me, when ye shall search for me with all your heart. Jeremiah 29v12-13

25 It is of the LORD's mercies that **we** are not consumed, because his compassions fail not. They are **new** every morning: great is thy **faithfulness**. The LORD is my **portion**, saith my soul; therefore will I **hope** in him. Lamentations 3v22-24

26 For thus saith the LORD GOD; Behold, I, even I, will both **search** my sheep, and **seek** them out. Ezekiel 34v11

27 But Daniel purposed in his **heart** that he would not defile himself with the portion of the king's **meat**, nor with the **wine** which he drank: therefore he requested of the prince of the eunuchs that he might not **defile** himself. Daniel 1v8

28. When Israel was a child, then I **loved** him, and called my son out of **Egypt**. Hosea 11v1

29. And it shall come to pass afterward, that I will pour out my **spirit** upon all **flesh**; and your sons and your **daughters** shall prophesy, your old men shall dream dreams, your young men shall see **visions**: Joel 2v28

30. Seek **good**, and not evil, that ye may live: and so the LORD, the God of hosts, shall be with you, as ye have spoken. Amos 5:14

Bible verses 4 answers.

31 Though thou exalt thyself as the eagle, and though thou set thy nest among the stars, thence will I bring thee **down**, saith the **LORD**. Obadiah 1v4

32 And God saw their works, that they turned from their **evil** way; and God repented of the evil, that he had said that he would do unto them; and he did it **not**. Jonah 3v10

33 He hath shewed thee, O man, what is **good**; and what doth the LORD require of thee, but to do justly, and to love **mercy**, and to walk **humbly** with thy God? Micah 6v8

34 The LORD is **good**, a strong hold in the day of trouble; and he knoweth them that trust in him. Nahum 1v7

35 The Sovereign Lord is my **strength**; He makes my feet like the feet of a **deer**, He enables me to go on the heights. Habakkuk 3v19

36 The Lord thy God in the midst of thee is mighty; he will **save**, he will rejoice over thee with joy; he will rest in his love, he will joy over thee with **singing**. Zephaniah 3v17

37 The silver is **mine**, and the **gold** is mine, saith the LORD of hosts. Haggai 2v8

38 And he shewed me Joshua the high priest standing before the angel of the **Lord**, and Satan standing at his right hand to resist him Zechariah 3v1

39 For I am the LORD, I **change** not; therefore ye sons of Jacob are not consumed.

Malachi 3v6

Solutions to the Prophets Crossword Puzzle 1

2J	O	N	7A	H
			M	
		5O	B	A	3D	I	A	4H
		S		A				O
			6J		N			S
			O		I			E
			1E	Z	E	K	I	A	L
			L		L			

Across

1. Which prophet is known for prophesying about the valley of dry bones.
2. Which book speaks about the prophet who was swallowed up by a great fish?
5. Who wrote the shortest book the old testament?

Down

3. Which prophet was thrown into the lions den?
4. Which prophet was told to mary a woman who would not be faithful to represent Israel and its behavior toward God?
6. Which prophet was most famous for being quoted by Apostle Peter on the day of Pentecost?
7. Which book that was written by a prophet has only 9 chapters?

Solutions to Prophets crossword puzzle 2

				6Z		3H		
1B				E		A	2N	
E				C		B	A	
T			7M A L A C H I	H		A	H	
H				R		K	U	
L	5H A G G A I			I		K	M	
E				A		U		
H						K		
4Z E P H A N I A H						U		
M						K		

Across

4. Which book spoke about the day of the lord more than any other old testament book and the prophet prophesied during the reign of Josiah, the king of Judah?

5. Which book in the old testament written by a prophet only has two chapters?

7. Which book is the last book in the old testament?

Down

1. Which book has prophesy about the birth of Christ?

2. Which book has only 3 chapters?

3. Which book is very difficult to pronounce?

6. Which book is the second to last book in the old testament?

Solutions to Creation Cross Word Puzzle

```
                              10A  B   8E  L
                                       V
  2D      9C      4H  5E  A   V   E   N
  7A  D   A   M       A
  Y       I           6R  E   S   T
      3N  I   1G  H   T
              O       H
              D
```

Across

3. What did God call the darkness?
4. What did God call the firmament?
6. What did God do on the seventh day?
7. What was the name of the first man?
10. Who killed Abel?

Down

1. Who said let there be light and there was light?
2. What did God call the light?
5. What did God call the dry land?
8. What was the name of Adam's wife?
9. What was the name of Adams first son?

Solutions to Noah Crossword Puzzle

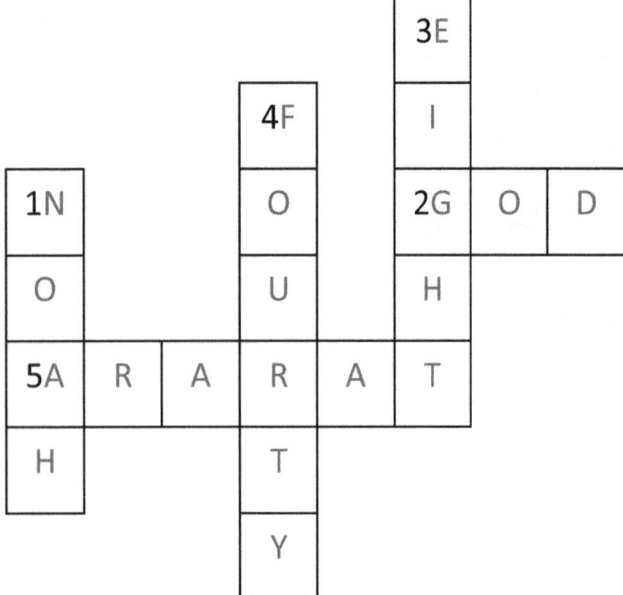

Across
2. Who shut the door of the ark?
5. What is the name of the mountain that Noahs ark rested on?

Down
1. Who built the ark?
3. How many people were saved in the ark?
4. How many days and nights did it rain?

Solutions to Abraham Crossword Puzzle

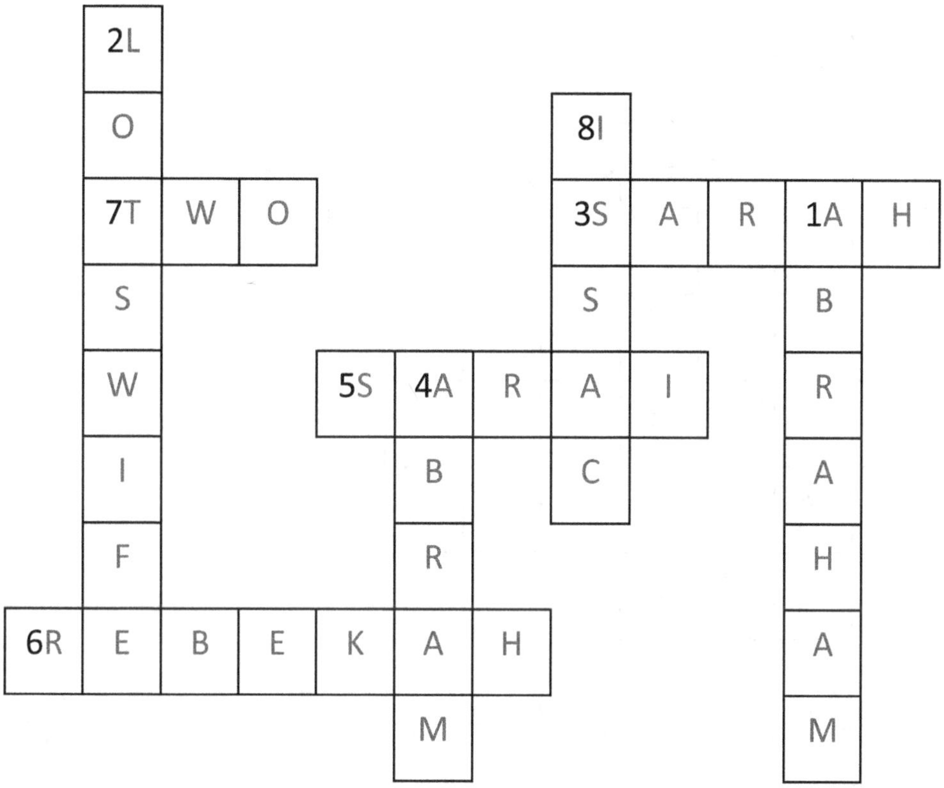
2L
O
8I
7T W O
3S A R 1A H
S
S
B
W
5S 4A R A I
R
I
B
C
A
F
R
H
6R E B E K A H
A
M
M

Across

3. Who was Abraham’s wife?
5. What was Sarah's name before it was Sarah?
6. Who was Isaac's wife?
7. How many children did Isaac have?

Down

1. Who is the father of many nations?
2. Who was turned into a pillar of salt?
4. What was Abraham's name before it was Abraham?
8. Who was the father of Jacob and Esau

Solutions to Jacob's Crossword Puzzle

```
                    8B
              3O  N  E        5L
      7I              N        E        4T  W  O
       S              J        A         W
       R         6R   A  C  H  A  E  L
       A              M                  L
      1G  E  N  E  S  I  S              V
       L              N        E
```

Across

1. Which book in the bible is the story of Jacob seeing a ladder?

3. How many daughters did Jacob have?

4. How many wives did Jacob have?

6. What's the name of Jacobs second wife?

Down

4. How many sons did Jacob have?

5. What's the name of Jacobs first wife?

7. What was Jacob's name changed to?

8. What was Jacob's last son's name

Solutions to the Bible Quiz

1	G	What is the first book in the new testament?	⟶	Matthew
2	C	What is the last book in the bible?	⟶	Revelation
3	H	Who wrote Genesis to Deuteronomy?	⟶	Moses
4	E	Who wrote the book of Ezra?	⟶	Ezra
5	D	Who wrote the book of Nehemiah?	⟶	Nehemiah
6	K	Who wrote most the book of Psalms?	⟶	David
7	A, B, J	Who wrote the songs of Solomon?	⟶	Solomon
8	A, B, J	Who wrote the Ecclesiastes?	⟶	Solomon
9	A, B, J	Who wrote proverbs?	⟶	Solomon
10	I	Who wrote Isaiah?	⟶	Isaiah
11	F	Who wrote Jeremiah and Lamentation?	⟶	Jeremiah
12	L	Who wrote the book of Ezekiel?	⟶	Ezekiel

Solutions to the Bible Quiz 2

1	Who wrote the book of Daniel?	Daniel	A
2	Who wrote the book of Hosea?	Micah	B
3	Who wrote the book of Joel?	Habakkuk	C

4	Who wrote the book of Amos?		Amos	D
5	Who wrote the book of Obadiah?		Zephaniah	E
6	Who wrote the book of Jonah?		Zechariah	F
7	Who wrote the book of Micah?		Jonah	G
8	Who wrote the book of Nahum?		Obadiah	H
9	Who wrote the book of Habakkuk?		Haggai	I
10	Who wrote the book of Zephaniah?		Hosea	J
11	Who wrote the book of Haggai?		Joel	K
12	Who wrote the book of Zechariah?		Nahum	L
13	Who wrote the book of Malachi?		Malachi	M

Solutions to the Bible Quiz3

1	A	Who wrote the book of Daniel?	⟶	Daniel
2	J	Who wrote the book of Hosea?	⟶	Hosea
3	K	Who wrote the book of Joel?	⟶	Joel
4	D	Who wrote the book of Amos?	⟶	Amos
5	H	Who wrote the book of Obadiah?	⟶	Obadiah
6	G	Who wrote the book of Jonah?	⟶	Jonah
7	B	Who wrote the book of Micah?	⟶	Micah
8	L	Who wrote the book of Nahum?	⟶	Nahum
9	C	Who wrote the book of Habakkuk?	⟶	Habakkuk
10	E	Who wrote the book of Zephaniah?	⟶	Zephaniah
11	I	Who wrote the book of Haggai?	⟶	Haggai
12	F	Who wrote the book of Zechariah?	⟶	Zechariah
13	M	Who wrote the book of Malachi?	⟶	Malachi

Solutions to Old Testament word Scramble

1. GISEESN   G E N E S I S

2. XOSDUE   E X O D U S

3. VIILECTSU   L E V I T I C U S

4. MEUSNRB   N U M B E R S

5. OTNEOUREYMD   D E U T E R O N O M Y

6. HOSAUJ   J O S H U A

7. DSEUJG   J U D G E S

8. UTRH   R U T H

9. USA1LEM   1 S A M U E L

10. E2AMSLU   2 S A M U E L

11. GKI1NS   1 K I N G S

12. N2KIGS   2 K I N G S

13. HELNIRS1OCC   1 C H R O N I C L E S

14. LRICSCN2OHE   2 C H R O N I C L E S

15. ZARE   E Z R A

16. NHEEAHIM   N E H E M I A H

17. EEHTRS   E S T H E R

18. BJO   J O B

19. PASMLS   P S A L M S

20. RPSROBEV   P R O V E R B S

Solutions to matching

1	I David	⟶	Which brave young boy had a fight with a giant called Goliath?
2	D Noah	⟶	Who did God give the job of building a massive boat called an ark?
3	F Delilah	⟶	What was the name of the lady who was married to the strongest man?
4	G Jonah	⟶	Who got swallowed by a whale?
5	B Adam and Eve	⟶	Which man and woman lived in the Garden of Eden?
6	E Daniel	⟶	Who was thrown into a den of lions by an evil King?
7	A Jacob and Esau	⟶	Can you name a set of twin boys?
8	H Solomon	⟶	Who was known as the Wise King?
9	C Benjamin	⟶	Who was Joseph's younger brother?
10	J 10. Egypt	⟶	10. Where was Moses born?

Solution to

1	G	Shepherd	---→	What "job" did David have as a boy?
2	H	Jonathan	---→	Who was David's best friend?
3	D	God's promise to not flood the earth ever again.	---→	What was the meaning of the rainbow in the sky?
4	I	Genesis	---→	Which is the first book of The Bible?
5	F	Harp	---→	What instrument did David play?
6	C	Proverbs	---→	Which book of The Bible is full of wise sayings?
7	J, E	Moses	---→	Who was given The Ten Commandments from God at the top of a mountain?
8	A	Cain	---→	Who killed his brother?
9	E, J	Moses	---→	Who made a bronze snake?
10	B	Light	---→	What did God create on the first day of creation?

Solutions to the Old Testament word scramble

1. GISEESN

   G E N E S I S

2. XOSDUE

   E X O D U S

3. VIILECTSU

   L E V I T I C U S

4. MEUSNRB

   N U M B E R S

5. OTNEOUREYMD

   D E U T E R O N O M Y

6. HOSAUJ

   J O S H U A

7. DSEUJG

   J U D G E S

8. UTRH

   R U T H

9. USA1LEM

   1 S A M U E L

10. E2AMSLU

    2 S A M U E L

11. GKI1NS

    1 K I N G S

12. N2KIGS

    2 K I N G S

13. HELNIRS1OCC

    1 C H R O N I C L E S

14. LRICSCN2OHE

    2 C H R O N I C L E S

15. ZARE

    E Z R A

16. NHEEAHIM

    N E H E M I A H

17. EEHTRS	ESTHER
18. BJO	JOB
19. PASMLS	PSALMS
20. RPSROBEV	PROVERBS

Solutions to the Old Testament word scramble

1. HNEHAEMI	NEHEMIAH
2. REETHS	ESTHER
3. JBO	JOB
4. LSPSMA	PSALMS
5. RSOBVEPR	PROVERBS
6. SLESTCCASEIE	ECCLESIASTES
7. OGLSSOONNFOOM	SONGOFSOLOMON
8. AAISIH	ISAIAH
9. JREMEAHI	JEREMIAH
10. INNLAOMEATTS	LAMENTATIONS
11. IKEEEZL	EZEKIEL
12. IDANEL	DANIEL
13. AEOHS	HOSEA
14. LOEJ	JOEL
15. OAMS	AMOS

16.	ABODAHI	O B A D I A H
17.	OJHAN	J O N A H
18.	CHIAM	M I C A H
19.	AHMNU	N A H U M
20.	AKBHKKUA	H A B A K K U K
21.	ZHIHAAENP	Z E P H A N I A H
22.	GAAIHG	H A G G A I
23.	HZEHACIAR	Z E C H A R I A H
24.	MHLAAIC	M A L A C H I

A	B	C	D	E	F	G	H	I	J	K	L	M	N	O	P	Q	R	S	T	U	V	W	X	Y	Z
88	68	72	66	78	76	80	69	65	71	70	83	73	81	84	89	77	75	90	79	67	85	82	74	86	87

O B A D I A H
84 68 88 66 65 88 69

J O N A H
71 84 81 88 69

M I C A H
73 65 72 88 69

N A H U M
81 88 69 67 73

H A B A K K U K
69 88 68 88 70 70 67 70

Z E P H A N I A H
87 78 89 69 88 81 65 88 69

H A G G A I
69 88 80 80 88 65

Z E C H A R I A H
87 78 72 69 88 75 65 88 69

M A L A C H I

73 88 83 88 72 69 65

Solutions to Bible quiz 1

1		How many books are in the old testament?	39
2		How many books are in the new testament?	27
3	E	What is the last book in the old testament?	Revelations
4	B, J	Which book in the bible has the creation story?	Genesis
5	C	What is the longest book in the bible?	Psalms
6	B, J	What is the first book in the bible?	Genesis
7	G	What is the second book in the bible?	Exodus
8	D	What is the third book in the bible?	Leviticus
9	F	What is the fourth book in the bible?	Numbers
10	H	What is the fifth book in the bible?	Deuteronomy
11		How many books are in the bible?	66

Solution to Women of the Bible

```
                                        10R                8J
                      16S          7H  A   N   N   A   H
        9M  I   R   I   A   M           C                  E
                      R    11L 4E  A   H                   L
                      A         V  [ ]  A        15N
  5D  E   B   O   R  1A  H     13R  E   B   E   K   A   H
  E                   S         A            L            O
  L                  3E  S   T   H   E  14R               M
2D  I   N   A   H     N         A        U                I
  L                   A         B        T
  A                   T                  H
  H                   H
```

Across

2. _____ is the seventh child and only daughter of Jacob and Leah.

3. _____ risked her life to save her people (the Jews), and it pays off.

5. _____ was a prophet and judge who people frequently came to for guidance.

Down

1. " She was an Egyptian princess, aristocratic, and high-born. Pharaoh honored Joseph by giving him ___ as his wife.

4. God creates _____to be of help to Adam.

5. _____ name means "delicate" or "dainty one. The Philistines approach Delilah and offer to pay

7. Hannah was barren until she meekly asked for a son from God, promising that she would dedicate him to His service.

9. _____ is the elder sister of Aaron and Moses. She suggests to Pharaohs daughter that a Hebrew woman nurse baby Moses and thereby reunites Moses with his mother.

11. She was Jacob's first wife, who was deceptively given to him after he had worked for seven years

13. She is married to Isaac and is the mother of Jacob and Esau.

her handsomely if she is able to find out why Samson is so strong.

8. _____ killed the man who had oppressed the Israelites for 20 years.

10. Rachel was Jacob's second wife and his true love. She died in childbirth.

13. Joshua sends two spies into Jericho to scope out the situation. The spies find their way to hers house and she hides the men at great risk to herself.

14. _____ swears an oath, saying she will remain with Naomi.

15. Ruth and _____ both experience the loss of loved ones. ___ was Ruth's mother--in-law

16. _____ was Abraham's wife. Amazingly, she had a child—Isaac—at the ripe old age of 90.

Solutions to the Creation to the Flood Cross-word Puzzle

```
        5M
6J   A   R   E   D              2S        9L
     H                    4K   E   N   A   N
     A                         T        M        1A
     L   10N      7E   N   O   C   H    E        D
     A   O        N                     C        A
     L   A        O              11S   H   E   M
8M   E   T   H   U   S   E   L   A   H
     L
```

Across

4. – son of Enosh, grandson of Asam
6. – father of Enoch
7. – son of Jared who was taken up to God without dying
8. – son of Enoch, grandfather of Noah
11. – Noah's oldest son and original ancestor of Israel.

Down

1. – first man
2. – third son of Adam and Eve
5. – son of Kenan, descendant of Seth
7. – son of Seth, grandson of Adam
9. – father of Noah
10. – last of the ten antediluvian Patriarchs and hero of the Flood

Solutions to the line of Cain Cross-word Puzzle

	2E							5I				
	V							R				
7M	E	T	H	U	S	A	E	8L				
E					D			1A	D	A	M	
H								M				
U				3C				E				4E
J		9T	U	B	A	L	-	C	A	I	N	
A				I				H				O
E				N								C
L												H

Across
1. – first man
7. – "man of God", descendant of Cain
9. – son of Lamech

Down
2. -First woman
3. – firstborn son of Adam
4. – son of Cain
5. – son of Enoch
7. – son of Irad
8. – fifth descent from Cain, rude and ruffianly, with him the curtain falls on the race of Cain

Solutions to After the Flood Cross-word Puzzle

							4H			5S		
	9F					13R	A	C	H	A	E	L
2N	O	A	H				M			R		
	T						14I	S	A	A	C
12L	H		15L				S		H		
10R	E	B	E	K	A	H		8S	R		
A		R	■	B		3A	B	R	A	H	A	M
H		7J	A	C	O	B		L		E	
			N			R		T		L	
		11E	S	A	U				,	
			M							
			.							

Across

2. ___father of Shem.
3. __father of multitude", the first Hebrew patriarch, son of Terah,
7. ___ original ancestor of the nation of Israel and father of the 12 ancestors of the 12 tribes of Israel.
10. __ wife of Isaac
11. ___ twin brother of Jacob
13. ___ second wife of Jacob

Down

3. ___name was changed to Abraham
4. __ brother of Shem
5. ___ Abraham's wife
8. Lot's wife was turned into a pillar of ___
9. Isaac was the ___of Jacob and Esau
12. __ was the first wife of Jacob
14. Jacob's name was changed to ___ shortly after the signing of the

14. ___ only son of Abraham by Sarah and patriarch of the nation of Israel

historical treaty (which split Israel from the East)

15. ____ was Jacob's father in-law

Solutions to After the flood part 2

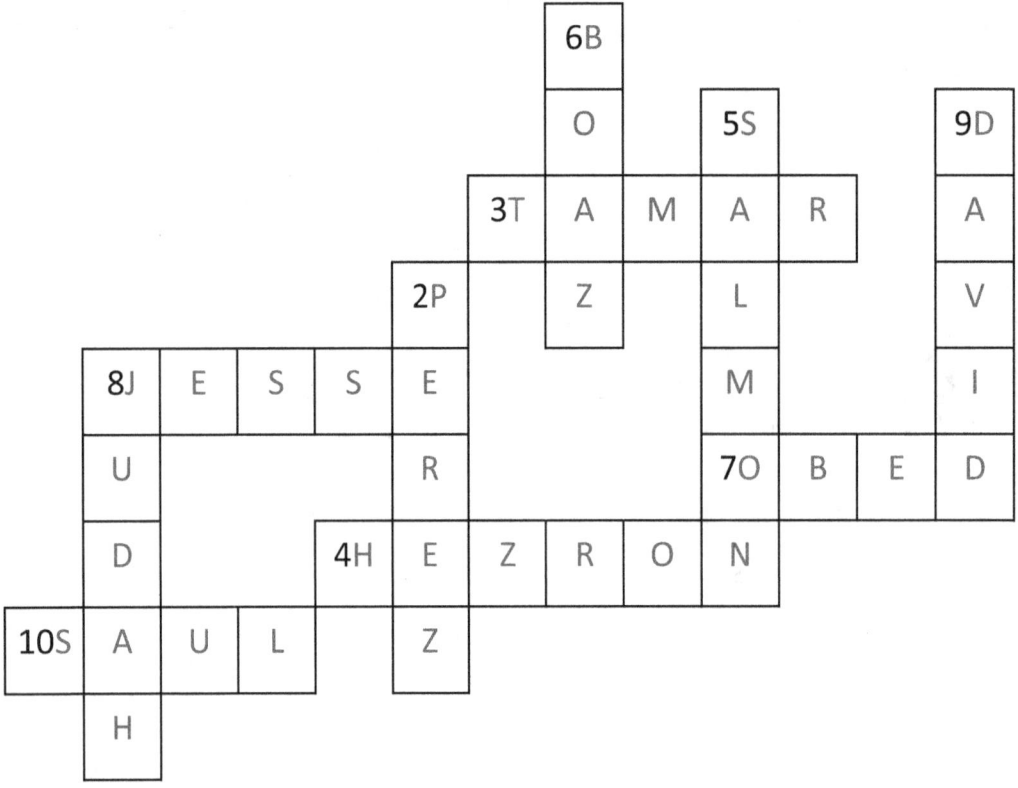

Across

3. ; Judah's daughter in law .
4. – great grandson of Jacob
7. – son of Boaz and Ruth, father of Jesse, grandfather of King David
8. – father of King David
10. ___ first King of Israel, he was king before David

Down

2. – one of the twins born through the illicit affair between Judah and his daughter-in-law,
5. – father of Boaz
6. – married Ruth and became Obed's father (David's grandfather)
8. – fourth son of Jacob and progenitor of the tribe of Judah
9. – killed Goliath

Solutions to The Twelve Tribes of Israel Cross-word Puzzle

13R	8E	U	B	E	N		12N			3B							
	P						2A	S	H	E	R						
	H						P			N							
	R	10J	U	D	A	H	H			J							
	A						T		5G	A	D						
	6I	S	14S	A	C	H	A	R		M				15Z			
	M		I				L			1I	S	R	A	E	L		
			M				I			N				B			
7J	O	S	E	P	H									U			
			O											11L	E	V	I
	9M	A	N	A	S	S	E	H						U			
												4D	A	N			

Across

1. Twelve Tribes of _____ (sons of Jacob, aka Israel)
2. ♣ – eighth son of Jacob and Zilpah
4. – fifth son of Jacob and the first son born to Jacob by Rachel's maid Bilhah,
5. – seventh son of Jacob and Zilpah and founder of the Tribe of Gad
6. ♣ – ninth son of Jacob, fifth born by Leah
7. _taken to Egypt as a slave, eventually became interpreter of the pharaoh's dreams

Down

3. ♣ – twelfth and last born of Jacob's sons
8. – second and youngest son of Joseph and Asenath
12. – sixth son of Jacob by his concubine Bilhah
14. – second son of Jacob of Leah

9. ♣ – son of Joseph and Asenath and founder of the Tribe of Menasheh

10. – fourth son of Jacob and founder of the Tribe of Judah

11. – third son of Jacob and Leah

13. – first son of Jacob and Leah, founder of the Tribe of Reuben

15. – tenth son of Jacob and sixth by Leah

Reference

KJV Reference Bible (2010) Holdman Bible Publishers

I hope you enjoyed this quick tour through the New Testament

Other workbooks available include:

A Quick Tour Through the Bible Part 2

The Creation Story

The life of Queen Esther

The Life of Jesus

The Self Esteem Work-book Part 1

The Secret to Anger Management; A guide to helping kids understand their emotions

Intimate Relationships: Activities I have used with couples for many years

The Secret to Weight Loss Workbook Part 1: Using Mindfulness & Hypnosis to Develop a Healthy Lifestyle

Comments

Please send comments or suggestions to
The Mind Heart & Soul Enrichment Center, PO Box 7990, Lawton, OK 73506 or you can
email me at mhscec@yahoo.com

Thank you very much.

www.ingramcontent.com/pod-product-compliance
Lightning Source LLC
Chambersburg PA
CBHW081407280526
45788CB00009B/3012